I Was Blown Back

I Was Blown Back

———————————

Norman Fischer

Singing Horse Press 2005

ISBN 0-935162-32-1
Singing Horse Press
3941 Gaffney Court
San Diego, CA 92130

Singing Horse Press titles are available directly from the publisher at www.singinghorsepress.com or from Small Press Distribution (800) 869-7553 or www.spdbooks.org.

Preface

These poems express directly as I could get it the concerns I have had and the problems and wonderings that occupy me probably always but especially in the years between 1999 and 2003 or so (I never date my poems, imagining them I suppose to exist in some extra-temporal zone, which is how it feels when I am writing them, as if the words were coming from elsewhere, or at least nowhere, and do not describe anything I have seen or experienced). Though I was born and happily raised Jewish, most of my adult life, about twenty-five years, I have functioned as a Zen Buddhist priest. Since the late 1980's I have been immersing myself, with increasing intensity, in the language, practices, and metaphors of my ancestors. Thanks to my close friend and teacher Rabbi Alan Lew, my collaborator in the Jewish meditation movement, I have been able to meet the Jewish sages of the past face to face, and to read the Torah with a sense that its hidden meanings touch the as yet unrecognized patterns, the tavnit, of my mind. Reading Paul Celan during this period also had a transformative effect on me. (Thanks to John Felstiner for his invaluable work on Celan). Of course Buddhist thought and practice remain crucial sources for me, as template for deciphering my own experience in meditation and in living. For a long time I felt my poetry and my religious practice as quite separate, but after a while I noticed that I was writing about intimate religious experience, although this had never been my intention. Like characters in a novel, or intimate friends, my poems seem to have minds of their own, and to draw me toward insights and intentions I would never have had if left to my own devices. The reader will find here many references, usually obscured, though not by design, to Buddhist and Jewish sources. As I do religious practice with people in many places I am often asked, "How is it possible that you are a Buddhist priest who also practices and teaches Judaism?" Why is this a question? To me there's no problem here and there could only be if one saw truth as propositional and therefore explainable, with one explanation somehow canceling or obviating another. But truth isn't anything, or, if it is anything it is a shifting shape, a feeling, not an explanation. And language—at least as far as I am interested in it—isn't so much a tool for communicating particular ideas as it is a meditation on human meaning's torqued mysteries. I suppose poetry has been the key for me to remaining more or less free of fixed ideas despite being a committed religious person. Poetry always raises more questions than it can answer. I hope religion does too.

Always a lot of friends die and this book remembers many who left the world during the time of its composition. My close friend, fellow Buddhist priest, and poetry Master Philip Whalen, first of all. Constantly missed. Maylie Scott, also a Buddhist priest and old friend. And the poet and publisher Gil Ott. The long poem "Ask a Difficult Question" was written in memory of my cousin Anne Wruble, a good woman who died too young in 1999, but with great courage. Many of the other poems in this volume are also meditations on death and time, which seem still immensely and unspeakably strange, always connected to one another, and my constant companions.

The poets Michael Palmer, Paul Naylor, and Hank Lazer read the manuscript of this book with loving generosity and made many valuable suggestions. I want to thank them for their help and ongoing support. I am old enough now to have enjoyed the long friendship of many poets who have inspired and encouraged my work. I am lucky to count the poets Leslie Scalapino, Lyn Hejinian, Bob Perelman, Charles Bernstein, Kit Robinson, Ron Silliman, Denise Newman, Steve Benson, Carla Harryman, Barrett Watten, and Lewis Hyde among them. And many others. Through them I've learned that poetry is community, in the deepest sense. I also owe a great personal debt to the important avant garde poet Jackson Mac Low, who passed away in 2005.

Some of these poems appeared in the literary magazines *Facture, Crayon, Tin Fish, Nocturnes (Re)view,* and *Bombay Gin.* My thanks to the editors of these publications for their support of my work, and for their persistent efforts in publishing poetry that attempts to mine language's depths, and that would never see the light of day without them.

Also thanks to Marc Lesser, who, as creative director of Brushdance, chose the Rumi quotations that appeared in a blank book he gave me, in which "Ask a Difficult Question" was written. Thanks again to Hank Lazer who found the Lyotard quotation that serves as one of the epigraphs for this book.

I offer this book in dedication to my wife Kathie Fischer. How odd and intimate to live a daily life with someone a long time, keeping love going, recognizing how little we really know of another. Or of one's self for that matter.

Norman Fischer
Charlotte's Way
Muir Beach, California
February 2005

"But how can we not recognize that there was also this little trickle of voice and thought continuing to say: Listen, to be or not to be, that is not the question. What the question is, is: What has been asked of us? What can one do to be just with regard to this breath of which we are the guardians? We have been blown away! – in every sense."

—Jean-Francois Lyotard

"The blare of the horn grew louder and louder. Moses spoke and God answered him in thunder."

—Exodus. 19:19.
Trans. Jewish Publication Society

I

I Was Blown Back

A thousand people contained within a lit square
Three trees silhouetted straight up branching eerily out

Ordinary clouds stream against the fluted airways—
How their smoky fingers make music against the dark

Quietly what's good
Descends like dust
Or dusk onto the milky landscapes

The people stand still
And all around them
The bluster of their thinking
Pulls down lightning from above
And the platforms rattle

The owls in the trees scatter their nocturnal alarms—
How decisive the universal defeat

It isn't that the ending came first
A cloudy picture having circulated so long in air
You could doctor it, ordering it around with the wind
So it did not seem there was a final truth

Looking into the mirror see a mirror
Reflective as snow wanting to fall up
Into history's self conscious play-by-play
Whose limit approaches me as prophecy

Astonishing to think the old tales
Are not kidding — like organelles
They stick themselves onto larger questions
That come later and feed them

The motivation's wrong
Which belief controls it?
In the end hearing is reflexive

No machine can register
What's only proposed

In the bonds there's blood
In collaboration wine
No longer seeking the horizon
You're awash in the plumes of your closeted longing
Blind to the elongating scenery

You were saved from drowning long ago
By a woman from a foreign family
And now you are paying the price of endlessness
For which you have been given an unsayable letterless name

Your fate was sealed when you first felt the torture
Of being
Displaced, flesh condensed simply because
It could be

I'm not sure of this
So I put my head down
In the desert
On a pillow of stone
See a pillar of smoke
Obscuring the tombs behind my eyes

I go on like this for a long time if only for a moment
Bound and free
Not arriving—

Prematurely safe
In the illusion of my life

Head straight for the decision points
Eliminate the detail in between
None of that makes a person—

Everything's displacement
Condensation of expansive defeat coils
Right there in the poached center

Is the starting pad—
Let fling the extras
Where the point meets the exile

There's forgetting
It's up to someone else
To interpret your life

They've got it in their pockets like lint—
Turn your head that way—
Don't try to remember any of this

I can already read my mind

No matter how easily arranged
A collar may be around a neck
There's a limit to their fineness
That can't be fitted
To a form of thought that suits it

And for which it suffers
These are sure-footed words
Nor is it entirely a matter of interest
I have waited very long for this answer
It is not the one I expected

God's distance—how drink it in
If not in time's water—
Refreshment for going up the tower

Standing there three days gazing
At nothing you could reach
Obliterating the hours in images

Here on the tower
You can't see the tower
But someone mentions it to you in a whisper

Now's the time
To fling fire, scatter air, break stone
Dissolve all faith and knowledge —
Get the beginning back, never cower

In eyes words spill
Thought dissolves in water
Unstable, overflowing its lips
Lapping quiet out beyond the breakers

There's casting up of weight in the swell
So that looking into the depths there's no contact
Outside the sheer warmth that that is there

A presence in the larger vicinity
Is immanent collision
A force pressing over you unannounced
Of memory as far back as the beginning

Carried along in the effortless floating
Sky and sea sketch out an edge
That you reach for with your hand
Making mere gestures within the sounds of the words

Waves sound like tinkling glass on the beaches
My eyes cupped with light so deep back
There's no connecting, no escape

I suffered through this day of unhappiness
For these few word-scraps whose limitations
Are drawn along the lengthening borders
Of the soul-region called "word"
So my attention averts from it
Laughing out loud swiveling around toward it

How hard I work
To open locks for which there seem to be no keys
Stranded here as usual beside the pump
While the social body blunders on in the forced march of
        its deceptions
Toward a lurching just maybe possible dream
That seems to saturate my soul like starch in a shirt
But always comes to nothing when I can't wake up

No matter how hard I try to assign myself to something
I keep floating free in chunks
Always elusively elsewhere
Which turns out to be a newer version of the same thing
        but in different words
So I can never get used to the feeling of what I am

Still, planes take off into sky
The way you imagine something that might occur tomorrow
That won't quit once you start in on it
Nor blow up properly when the fuse is lit
Giving life that razor's edge quality

Singing my destiny, hard to hold in hand
Otherwise than in what's made up—
Stories echo down the stairwell to the laboratory basement
Where in the distillery they're refined and retooled
Till I lift my cup of clear water up to the light
Which intoxicates as much as fire does—

Assemble the letters with care
Written, carved, balanced precariously
Atop one another as weighty blocks
Until one topples down into the heart-forests
Where speech ceases to be a babble
And the animals creep back into my dreams

That love's lidless
Like a tree that falls down all over again
Roots dangling in thin air—the heart's gripless
Attachment

The rain never lets up
Falling uselessly into the sea

Nor do I not speak my mind in the words I employ
Intending to go left my letters veer right
Fall in lines where I wish to rise

The body takes no orders
Its nature is to be disturbed
Molested, corrupted, folded
Into a priceless perfection
As the motion of a wave

Released like the spray
Hazed out in minute momentary droplets
By the force of a breaker on a rock

Such birds as are barely seen in thick air
Fly by in the novels of my life
Dreams whose meaning I dream
For my doctor for his cure

It's hard to determine the temperature of anything—
Are these frozen raindrops clinging to my beard
Warmer than the ocean spray
Sliding down the backs
Of the tropical pelicans?

A new universe, massive, extensive, very far away...

The pine tree's patient in the driving rain
Without enervation or articulation
It does not weave a colorful tale of doom

Like a hand reaching back for a pillow
Like a ghost-written autobiography
It gorgeously gives itself away
To the mixed up signals of a parallel evening
Neither stopping nor stooping as I do
Willingly rooted and collapsed

Too late, too late the snow so well designed
Those snowflakes turning all around in the cold
The bloated feeling the world sometimes gets
When it has had its fill of snowflakes, they are so perfect

These words have been dictated to me
But in the buildings where the holy ones lie shattered
Who do not know how holy they are
And so prefer the evil they can do
In a day
All that I feel and know flayed and laid out on the table
Like rich meats at a buffet that bear no evidence
Of their bloody past and do not foretell a good future

I am not so sure I prefer peace to war
Happiness to the misery of danger and uncertainty
But in this storm among the living
The tidy trees at the crests of the mountains
Stand steady in the blasts from beyond

They are neither worried nor knowledgeable
So why should I be?

Time goes slow when you're desperate
Someone throws one fish into the boat, flopping
And the imaginary dream-worlds you usually live in,
Gauzy structures like sticky webs of time
In the middle of apparently persistent objects that wave
            among them like seaweed
Dissolve in a farrago of groping limbs—
Ah how hopeless it is, this haystack search
For the bright needle of self restoration—
Like rehabilitating an antique table, over and over you buff
The past to remove stains and scratches, produce a sheen,
But it's not working: memory's a deception
As is any organized notion of the person you are
That falls with the weight of what happens
Should the organs of perception ever actually tote the heft
…

What was that I just saw swimming by?

Nobody dreams of camels
At least not here where we dream of baboons
An elephant is likely to arrive to upset the arrangements
Followed by an old song that rhymes

However you remember, the days get exchanged
Morning for noon evening or night
As the dear years run like egg yolks
Bald and slow

The trees seem thin
In winter sucking up their juices from the frozen ground
More fortunate than the thronging crowd
That starves each year and dies alone

And even in your sorrow the known arrives
Like a prepared meal delivered warm
From a great distance

You are not hard of hearing
Standing before that massive carved stone
Wailing the wail of your people

Getting thrashed clean
Like clothes beaten on a stone
Squeezed and hung to dry

Your life flaps in the gusty breezes
And once in a while like a skiff
Sails pretty away on the blue

(In memoriam, Gil Ott, 1950—2004)

Not at all according to doctrine
I take orders
From order—or does order
Order the word
A secondary order outside the order
That conforms and binds?

This is how it is is not that
Only standard order prescribes notation
For a model to be named later
That has no function
In a living precious world

Because you expected them
To deliver what they seemed to ship
To match an inspired but contorted vision
Cloud-like in the world
You grow dark, disturbed
Stalk long corridors close to walls
Dart outside buildings
Into cold streets
Constantly mad at the sky—

It will take you years to learn
Words are free of their intentions
Fluttering like flags
They are more hymns than contracts
Though they are never without promise

Because of the terror things are
Because a corpse floats but a stone sinks
And rests on the bottom
But a corpse is cast out
Because the mind soars, sinks, wallows, wanders
Because the heart aches, breaks, beats, swells with pride
Because you can't see yourself in a mirror
Which eats your face
Pulls your insides out
So that everyone thinks they know you
And casually pronounce your holy names
Because you think the night is dark
And the light of day defines objects in your room
You pick up, grasp, and break
Because the cards you shuffled and arranged
Float out to form a picture
Then scatter on a rolling lawn in front of a large house
When you arrive there
Someone calls you by a second name
And asks you to answer
For all this

People, do not suppose that being addressed
As a ball is addressed or a letter
Gives entitlement to a name and an appointment book
Still, in the designated day you'll say good-bye
Or hello and that single moment of greeting
Or falling away will stand still like the sun once did
In the sky of a book—little known lists are then procured
And the items on them pronounced—
Being neither dead not alive they have a tendency
To bolt—in both senses of the word

One life answers another
In the long conversation that's falling
Through the timbre of our reedy voices
Endless calling and answering
Like circulating winds spelling out our names
That later on we forget
Just when we most need to know them
So as to hold a world solid
But by then we no longer care
Because we're swimming,
Swimming and floating
And shore is just a word we thought we knew
Sibilance of wind calling us onward

Why not leave this world
Whose histories flip back and forth freely like leaves on a
        tree or in a book?

That anything at all occurs—is it by luck or fate I take my
        meal at this table
Or does my sighing against the floorboards
Merely signal the final end of gravity
As if it were a rainbow-promise of a peaceful future?

Yesterday snow, today white beaches—
So much that can be accomplished all of a sudden, my
        accidental desires
Materialized as if I had the power of an angel—

Lets go outside and play,
Dropping all analogies for the moment—
These things I want to say—they fill the available space—

Maybe it amuses me to know
And when I go into that arena
My thinking falls of its dead weight

Why isn't my hand now the same size
As I know it must be
Looking at it through water
Or in another condition of my eyes?

The body is me, isn't strange fruit
It's familiar and corruptible

But long habit links me to my ancestors
Only insofar as all the seas stir but not at once
Or at the same pace

The thought behind this is proper to its station
People speak of me and later on I answer

In the golden stage
They change the rules
They build hospitals to fix their eyes
And the miracle of a person
Flickers on and off
Like a toggle switch or a sunset
Nice might to ring the world
And there are islands out to sea
Where people's voices struggle
With every blessed day

Big open yellow country
Low hills mud huts women
Pounding grain
Tying twigs to make a basket
Also can be worn as a hat
Smoking pipe
Running long distances
In dry air

Notorious how I blather on
Telling this story not in incidents
But in half truths
This rug here: I've seen it before
This cup: familiar also
Ideal, perfect, discernible, neither particular nor
perishable

The Lord is my shepherd etc.
The cup's too full

They say a disciple to be a disciple
Must sense a beginningless past, an endless future
And be motivated by that
Sure-footed because of it
Every step, even here, first and last

This day's clear skies
Depend on yesterday's roiling clouds
Through which one flies
Ascending and descending

My son's not me my wife's
Not my sister there's no protection
Under the sun save to offer, cast off
All, intent and without tears

To get it back finally able to see
The pyramid lodged inside the eyeball
A hoary host of smoking guns
All one's deeds, words, come careening back

Into the sandstorm of belief retrenchments
Toiling through the days and nights
Among choices one's too feeble to understand
In the numbered chapters of someone's book

All that has been written and known
Is like a man smashing up a chair
That has been made long ago
And is no longer useful
So must be disposed of

Is a window streaked with dirt
Against the sun
Setting over the sea
In winter (there is no snow
That falls into the sea)

A nation fitfully fades
Into the soil from which it sprang
An image, an ideal, a word-scrap—
Aging wood
Floating on the waters

Wherever you look life takes shape
According to the looking

Did I eat something wrong?
Why do the questions demand this of me?

One word—a wonder
Rising up in the air
Or settling onto a branch

The world is a vice
A work of art, perfectly dense
Even in its pressure

In conversation all I need
Given, bitterness of age and disappointment
At what can't be explained
As the explanations grind on
To an eventual everlasting halt

Can I trust thinking that thoroughly?
If I needed a word
It would find me

No matter what
Should intention intervene, desire arise
We're sunk

Not that desire's a problem
Just that it reaches out (like an army in the night)
For nothing that's there
So's disappointed
Inevitably and gets mad—

Calm down
Look at the sea
To horizon's markings on the sky
It's only water
So easy on the eyes
You can float off as is customary
No one really knows where this is going—

No use giving speeches in an empty palace
Several of us can play this game too
Listen for their words:
Can you hear me calling?

The sun rises does not set
Sets does not return
Due to you whom I am addressing

The untranslatable words I intone
Could never reach you
Since you are stuck inside them
Like dinner parts between someone's teeth
Soft, hidden, dissolving, nutritious

Life's unhealthy, death's a drag
On the system's uplifting state
It is head of state
A mess with pomp and circumstance
Leader of the band that plays on

So small the space
Between cloud and cloud
Reduced world
In the instant between
Life's uncertainty
And death's indefinability

We go along this way
Just long enough to speak
About what we see
Outside this window

Immersed again in cloud
The mirror renders water
Gray, red, green, blue
And the dark land
Heavy and unmoving within it

How the mighty have fallen!
How much they have to dream about
Because what's out there's lost to them—
They dream in order to place themselves
Back inside their smoking bodies

This is the story of a people
A long and colorful saga
Of trembling and deadly proliferation
Whose cost is this doomful restraint—
The gradual creaky opening of a heavy door

Now that your baby is born and named
You sense the enigma of belonging
The responsibility of breathing
Into the diorama world
The unadorned dismemberment of your holy temple

Like a replacement joint in consciousness
A blessing is like a knee
In that in both cases
There's something bent, something joined
Something stolen, something spoken just once

Insofar as your birth is a gratuity
You must run
Miles uphill
Till you feel the sweat of your brow
Your spoken gratitude or praise
In the hazy columns
Like a pilgrim on four continents

There's a poison
On the other side of the house

Hard not to catch the drift
Like a light going on and off
Accidentally

Each thing happens
So as to break free
Of the sound of my voice
That the others are straining to hear

Probably there's an ocean out there howling
And a gull croaking its cloying displeasure
Alone on a beach

In this narrowness the social terror is evident
Like a kiss full of trees
Spaced out at a great distance from one another
And stationary clouds in an oval blue sky

Softness surrounds the body—
That and the faraway rumble of a heavy-duty vehicle
Plowing steadily if slowly onward

If memory is a house well laid out
With foundation stones on bedrock
Then sunlight blazing on the water
Is a stone drilled with tiny perfect holes
Full of spatial music

The people from the past
Line up front and center waving their figments
Like palm fronds on a tropical beach in a storm

The world's wealth is frozen memory
So many birds wheeling about in reaction to tides and breezes
A separate more perfect body pitched violently
Into a world it never acknowledged—

The pressure of that senseless hurt
Brings now to the East
Something that rumbles and attends
Though it's far too bright
To make out

Now quietly I think of learning
Flinging it out all around like rice grains
Like music on the cornet

If a soul's like milk to be poured out
Why not lean forward into it, letting the quiet
Absorb the tatters of the memory fabric
That will bring you back to perfect place
As if it were a verb tense wreaking havoc
In the breasts of beasts and birds

Such small hearts flutter so quickly as they pass
Like angels addressing our meals
Little perfect eyes amassing evidence
For some global argument deep among the throats

Many mounded islands
And a white mountain peak in the distance
Bright red skies at dusk

What child's voice
Pronounces these things to make them so?

Frost on grass and roofs
Icy chill in the soul, a word, a name
A Frenchman addressing me in a monotone

What a luxury it would be
To have an inner life
A few trees in a pot
A scrawled list of formerly used words
And music, plenty of music,
That tinkles down the stairs like water
Or tiny shards of ice falling off melting roofs
Not to have to worry about the many arrangements
That go to shore up a life
It would be a pleasure to sink into those waters
And there would be no more images

The air talks to me in fluttering words
Birds in their patterns of flight
Earth underfoot relates her old tales
Reading these lines I crawl out to their edges
And gasp, returning, to be held again
In thrall to further thoughts
That fix my weight like a wire across the abyss—

Human mind's not human nature—

Looking out at landscape I hear the songs

Occupy your life, embrace it
Until there's no one around to explain

Quiet settles on the grasses
Like morning frost by the sea
Memory's time's graven image on the soul
A painting of isness' nonentity
An endless unreasonable sorrow you feel
In the enclosure of perception itself

In a finger snap the mind brightens
Time's trapdoor opens as the music plays

Never would be a measure
Of the feeling of knowing time

Of being bottled up within it

I was blown back
When someone called me by name
The one who yelled out loud
On separate occasions—
We all heard this distinctly

Such is tomorrow
Such the nameless name
Descending to depiction

There were eyes and ears but nothing to see or hear
Casting even the shadows into doubt
But there was light, light

Poetry proceeds by perfection—fits and starts—
Poetry proceeds by words

How I am is simple—
Just a word
That things roll in—
I know that
It's the shape
Their echo, reminder,
Their endless gentle streaming
Rocks me to sleep at night

I'm full, so my tears
Soak in the beauty of truth
And I'm blinking my eyes in the too bright
Night

So that
I think
I will turn away from where they think I am
To the place where you are—

To the salt water, the bread and the wine
The pleasure that rolls down the throat

In a white room
Bordered in green tile—
One red
Vase—how like
Sighing this is
The unfolding
Of genius upstarts that all of a sudden
Want to peel the world off itself
Banana skin without banana benefit
Revealing the implicated profit
Of nothing to defile

Now or never
Or now's never
Ever the case, cause
Of my eventual eternal
Return—how allow
Rain to fall some time
Seed grow, ripen, falter no more

About nothing
Always that
But a depth

Missing—copy, copy, copy—
The texts talk to each other
Hollering across history
Plowing through the centuries like tortured burden-earing
        mice

Cowering in the shadows, darting away
From every shaft of light—
Dwarfed by the covering stars

Ideas, the tomes
Went by I forgot
What it meant
Lost track of
The person I am
Not naming items in the room
I naturally faded
Was more fully embraced
By soft air

It's the old story told again
Lost in the brush of the sentence
Looking through the bars
At the invincible caged world—

Smoke rises up from the altars—
The soul's killed by seeing what is
Go down, meandering through being's deserts

No one talks to the dead anymore
They are lonesome there
Throwing off their clothing furiously
They hear the constant grinding of the wheel
What the government does is of no concern to them

Weeks go by—
The planets twirl in the sky's thin air

Las palmeras con cocos
In the tropical brilliance
By the sea—the ear lonely
In the fluctuating dream of you—

So the world is made
To disappear—

Let there be glow

What sort of planet is this
That is content to spin long in vastness
Lactating fitfully
Without ever once blushing
Or thinking to explain itself
And stands dependent
On the oligarchy of a handshake
In the sparkling webs of bluster and delight
The travesty of attraction and weight
That launches its ships in terrorist waves
Always sacramental in response

All's vacant—like a corner lot
Among weeds

But this space
Is not
Beaten back by what is
Rather turns and floats
Neither wondering nor retreating nor reflecting—
Spinning
Like any stone in air

Being old isn't—
The bodily sensations —
Are pleasant
Unpleasant
Interpreted in reference to memory
Obey the social contract of age,
Agreement, designation
Imputed on reading a face in the mirror
Which with advancing time
In reference to a fixture in the soul
Of self's melodious repetition
Is an object of questioning,
Searching look in eyes' brightness, chin's slump

All ages persist as one always
There's nor old nor young but additions
In the inventory of resignations
In the fact
Of the face
Or as the face
The silence in what comes and goes
In and out the opening

Mind like moon so new it's nothing
Then a shining sliver to a cool blast
Of suggestiveness. In the garden I wander
Or wonder for you are elusive and there's no
Trust short of nakedness and letting
Everything go away explicitly, embarrassingly
I put on these robes long ago not for the purpose
Of covering but to uncover
All these knots not for the purpose of
Untangling, which would be the end
But so as to set aflame, cool,
So that all float down while I watch
And leap and journey

You opened the gates
To speaking
So distance swallowed you—
The dangling words
Like columns of smoke
Ascending

Not trying to build a boat
Or threaten with a jawbone
You didn't materialize as someone
Which is a relief, only the body
Like soft fur pulsing
Constantly undulating air
Like a silky water-helmet
Flowing cool over a rock
Moves constant through the mist—
Being that but not knowing it
So you could say so
Other than jabbering
Broken-open syllables
Which sound beyond intelligibility
You pass through singing

(In memoriam, Philip Whalen 1923—2002)

Dreaming is better
For in dreams begin games
Whose rules are expandable
And interminable
Flowing through corridors of past and future
Which seep into the present
Like swamp water

Later on my letterhead
Will read this message in a bottle
In the middle of another dream
And say yes, I knew that man
Once

Slipped away
As memory
All over again
You're
Here—
A breath in
Then last out
Final crown
Of a lifetime's
Utter truth—

In being a person upright and tall
Noble and definite in speech
Never without a passion for what's right:

For the hopeless possible good enough world
That exists in our dreams—
Living and dying for that

(In memoriam, Maylie Scott, 1935—2001)

Don't know which way to go
With my sheep
It seems there are two of me
Or twenty-three—
How to guide them there
Which is anyway here
Is a sad joke
One drinks
Faithfully
Never revealing what's continually expressed
Though it wants to burst
And does, leaking in a thousand ways
For love of you

Dreaming is the least part of prophecy
And prophecy is revelation's nether shadow
Which is why we see the back
The curling clouds of vagueness
Not the crisp anterooms
In which throne-like furniture is stacked before the sideboard

Waking to face the weighty days
We carry on bravely within our structures
Forget entirely the contents and the clues
The notes, the tones, the sheet music—
Despite the hints embedded in words, syllables, phrases, metaphors
In the seen, heard, remembered and despised—

Thus we stir, stride on, stumble, trip, fall, and rise

I can't help it anymore—
My horses deliberately canter across the road
My armies march, my fishes swim
As I wait here for a bus

Everything's hollow, is smoke, glows
Like skin, like coal
Or milk, like silk
Like gloves, sacks, or gunfire
Towed along behind my heavier theories

Pride of distraction
Overcome by the sound of own voice
By the howling water's wind
A bridge to holiness
Real beyond desiring
What's true at first without thirst—

That's a chair's benefit—
The little incidents
From the past
That never happened
That I remember well
My many arms and cushions

Looking at you
I do see the trees move
I see those tender mottled boles—
The actors pass by—yes they too move me

Set apart—
A kiss against the forehead of what's not
Stray hairs on fate's upper lip
These things the animals don't bother to mention

How pleasurable writing is!
To stand
In the town hall's ballroom
With a winner of the Nobel Prize
To remember and record
Nothing if not now
In the telling
To ponder the strangeness
In silent utterance
Crossed out in time's text is
Certainly not worth leaving this world for
At least not sooner then the dinner's done
And the speeches have gone back to their tongues

I've lined up my things
Are the names of what I've got
Against which I am humble to gape

I can say I've walked this stony
Path one time
Conversed
With the worn things of my life
Not one accurately named
Not one emerging from the heart of the sky
My identity absorbs them all or they all it
My desire appears as a pillar of salt

Out from the narrowness of my thinking
I break onto an unsuspecting world

He who crosses God unintentionally
As someone crosses a street against the light
Is stoned to death
Or swallowed whole by the yawning earth

Which happens every time something falls
After it has been misplaced or forgotten
Gently dropped it falls
Without anyone's speaking of it

Gravity is God's chief notion
A spinning world with a heavy heart
The cup that is full will be drained
The empty cup filled
In accordance with the time and season
In accordance with weight and reason

Gratuitous love—how that's possible
The lifting love of women and men
That travels faster and further
Than feeling can muster—
The one who feeds you figs

Numbers shatter over pieces of being
Shower over water or dirt—

Words overheard
Talking into my thinking

What's my own?
Who asks?

A mother's anguish—
Yes that's so
Like a compass or a clock that presses on this pattern
Terror holding flesh in place—

How much of this is true?
How much painted?
Are these questions?
Is difference sensible?
What is one?

To love's to remember
What's held down
As release

On altars of stone
I sacrifice my thought—
See the smoke rising

No matter—illusion is good for you
It covers the head like a hat

Things must be alive—
In my hand are fingers
Rooted at the palm

Destiny's child
Proffers good manners
Offering a nine course chef's choice meal
Amid smoky decor
To indicate that the cresting waves
Rumble up deeply from below,
The secret lives of fishes

Life and death:
Adornments of the flesh

Place is code, perception collapses—
The whole heart stops—
The poor world
Shatters on a dime—you make it so
Snap the thread
Weep for the red
Release the unsaid
We've always been dead
We just need a little honey to get by on

I hang around
Seeking fodder for persuasion
Poured loosely it becomes music
That can't be repeated
And should never be allowed to leak out upon the earth
In these archetypal gestures of connection and betrayal—

Like a woman at the end of her rope,
It leans over the night fruit
Taking life in its two hands
Mixing up high and low
As if minds were highways without yellow center stripes

All that glitters is gold
Everything silent speaks

Poetry's a way not a topos
In which something appears
It's a sway among a swarm
To be hurled from side to side
Against the language walls
That tunnel subversive
Through what is
As far as it is known
Occasioning a gap in mind
Through which you could theoretically drive a truck

Meanwhile dogs bark and canaries tweet
Monkeys propend opposable thumbs
The covering sky won't shake out its stars
To cooperate with the head's coolness
The disaster that is human life on earth—

That this can be said (imagination
Blisters in the cauterized night)
Is possible only in the reams of paper
These hidden significant blotches of ink
We twiddle in the dark—

I know my fate rests with the embers

Seeing music, hearing trees, walking the talk back and forth
In the meadow's fuzzy flowers, mud
In the creamy peak's gray froth
In the demon soaring of a hawk
Knowing you can't just dismiss a whole people's bud
As if it was produce you didn't want to buy in the store

So I go around cities
Trying to climb out of the box I was born in
Watching out for pace, for strategy, for tintinnabulation
And lingering near the vestibule at the bottom of the stairs
Where the old drunk who works for me in the tailor shop
Pisses the night away, made oblivious by his sorrows

Is there anything new in this?
It's what the rabbis have been muttering about—
How being born and dying at its nub
Amounts to the same thing after all
Entering or leaving from or to the same spiral hole
And trying to say that's so, stuttering

I hear the sea washing the sky
Combing out the clouds' hair
As your hair is combed
By the beauty of your thinking—

If you are unsure
Do not shear—leave the camp
And in the desert ask
The important questions
And see who answers
When the bitter flavor trickles down the throat
Dissolving in the stomach's darkness

Forgive everything because nothing prevents you
From being a person—they only aid the cause
Gathered together in the twilight
Where amid the ringing of bells
You stop what you thought you were doing
And hold forth

II

Ask A Difficult Question

Variations on Rumi

In memoriam, Anne Wruble,
November 14, 1947—August 28, 1999

1.

Though we seem to be sleeping,
there is an inner wakefulness
that directs the dream,
and that will eventually startle us back
to the truth of who we are

Though there's a block in time
A blackness toward which the historical rock
Falls
(In its direction of names and dates
(In the photographs that are identified
(They are of people in a state
And in that dream of the possibility of now
Under hills that fold back against rivers
Anyone remembering the dream
Hears its sound
As systems of identity laid out on a table
In this small town remembering
Repeating
Which is a flourishing
Of a soft cloth which is knotted
In six places
Opening the book
The place where one lived
Actually something flitting along
That I thought I had
And came back here
That was gone there though it was exact
(Things changing, malls coming in
(Wide roads or the same roads and streets

(Hills where there were hills
(Trees where there were trees
(Spaces covered in grass where there were buildings
(Shops and houses, ordinary skies
Not connected to it
In the place where the battle was fought
And the river
(Now a wide expanse of calm light
(Beside broken trees
The river demanded or evoked
—this isn't some sort of dream
—this can't be any imitation
There is resonance between the times in the book
Which is carried about the room drunkenly
After sorrow and someone's death
That slants me back to where I am, startles

2.

Days full of wanting
Let them go by without worrying
that they do. Stay where you are
inside such a pure, hollow note.

Memory redactions are the mind's music
In the mind's mirror reflections of what's wanted, what is
No images
Only a smell
Of childhood
No one's parents
Coming along behind in round black cars

No one's photographs
Old clothing retrieved
Wanting is longing, distance
Means what's close appears far
As reaching out one's hand toward fruit
What's there recedes, disappears
(As the street curves
(As the old brick school
(Next to the white church
(The children entering
(In a freeze frame of long ago
Just remaining in that sound as if a bell
The present not disturbing the past
Settling into it like something falling into duff
The feeling of the ending included in the beginning
Everything mechanical approaching distance like a bell
Pure tone, water tone
(Road rises up behind the house
(Car climbs against the flat road and the hill
Journey, movement
But no characters
In the story
No forgiving framework
No persons, no personalities
Only struggle in the red tide of desperately
Losing what one built up
Like the water that rises falls back
Crashing
Against the thrusting up of the land
Taking the town and the buildings with it, streets
Buckling
Leaving debris and mud and breakage in its wake

(In the dream I wake to a feeling
(Not images only the feeling of the road climbing
(Humming sound of the tires
(Feeling what was incomplete
(My hand reached out for it but it was
(Dim, churned up, bloated fish floating in it
(And I could not advance only reach
But now there's something in it
The past isn't behind
Rather is mixed in like a color of paint
(A hump in the street next to the railroad track
(Beyond it the hill covered with trees
Some of the places I remember are gone
Encoded only in the body
That was the ghost they were
So that breathing the shadow
Those places grew brighter, reemerged
But the person speaking to me
Is gone as if she never were, also a dream
Her voice a mumble, can't make out words
But sense the speech as true
In the book those are the same words in the note
Words recalled
Or were embedded there
Black letters flaming on the white page
Indecipherable yet sweet
Farmland in gentle hills a code
The square fields in colors a code
The dividing trees enforcing a code
The only place to be in the words
As if the black lines
Crawling deliberately across the page

Were place enough
Persons whose passions are a code
Remember this
Suddenly flaps
A linen sheet or a cloth
Covering it so it's seen only as shape
That remains in motion
Unrecognizable only one knows it is there
Beneath
All what we speak of
Cleaning the table and the floor
Again
So many words again
Bodies and feelings again
Making something out of the world
The battle to defend the river
The fort that stood two years
Guns blazing and finally burned
(A stone marks that place
(Erected 1900
(As memory in the wedged corner of a front yard
(By the house on the river
(You go by there but do not know what this means

3.

Observe the wonders as they occur around you.
Don't claim them. Feel the artistry
moving through, and be silent.

No claim could be—that's a fallacy
Sun rises and in the night over the mountains

Bright yellow moon
Above the forest open space of glow
Above the house a room enchanted by light
Thirty years go by in the sun's coming
Going (No one's
(No thing's
(Going —earth's spin
(Also a fallacy,
(To be disproved later
(In the new mathematics
So a leaf opens out into the morning
Driving along old road to sun-soaked cloud
Two men greeting each other beside yellow tractor
The land unraveling hours and years
A change in weather
I think I remember the street
The cemetery there with all the people I remember
In it
Now as names
Now as dates
Walking up and down—is it the same grass
Or is it new grass
The iron of the fence we painted my father and I
(Who were alive at the time without work
(Sensations and thoughts
(Impressions and longings
The river flowing by impassively
Suggests somehow an open doorway, threshold
As if time's system were a flowing mirror image
Only much larger, mirror on mirror, lit
The mind a light turned around toward itself
So there's no other source of light (No

(Sun turning around in the sky
(Only the light diffusing everywhere but coming
(From nowhere, light inside the dense cocoons
(Hanging from the trees
So nothing to reach for
To want for in that sourceless light

4.

Keep knocking and the joy inside
will eventually open a window
and look to see who's there.

I am who returned to see
What's held in infirmity
In the gathering shadows
The grass a whisper
Or a rest
In the meaning of what's occurred one recognition
Small window overlooking the large yard
Small town on the river
To the west, to the east
Always across the river east and west
Street quiet
Some of the buildings that remain
And some gone replaced by roads
Or open spaces or grass
In imitation of a larger scope or pattern
Old people wandering by in sunlight
Across the landscape scars of cornfields
Beyond the house a hill

Beyond the railroad tracks
I did not notice then
No word for
The quiet joy of looking
No one's there to be doing this
No images in it
Only a slight fluttering of consciousness
Rustling of light, of a fluttering sheet
(Which is indescribable in another world
(That isn't elsewhere prior or exterior
(But in the obtuse organs like knots
(In a sheet of white cloth a pressure tortured
(World as seen among clouds from the air
(And also there is a pain in the left leg or in the back
(There is hair and a knot of muscle, breathing
And when there is that kind of loss
Having been led up to through long recognition
You expect her to walk in again through that door
Of the house
But she does not,
Will not—that is the kind of absence
It is
Decisive, like a vow
You hear her voice
Its timbre and inflection
Expressing notions
Of direction and passion
Logic of a life, of living
In the ear inside the mind
Not stimulated
By anything else
That comes from outside

The window
The lawn, the grass, the chair
As if she were there still in a wind you hear at night
Knocking against the house
As if it contained as a film on it
Thirty years of living—no cause for tears
No use for sadness
Because it makes no sense
This idea of loss
This decisive absence, this vocalization
Instead of anger and recrimination
Guilt and fury—information and image
(Banks along the river full of broken trees and brush
(Debris floating or weighted down with rocks
(Cocoons in the trees gray like moons suspended
(Houses in another world
(Red brick large school
(Labeled with a name
(It isn't
So find a book of mumbled words, find joy
In the tears in that
In the way reputation evokes shades of response
You have to listen for it in its tiny tappings
Against the pane (Now I have finally
(Begun
(Now have said have thought
(Have began at last—this occurs hundreds
(Of times, there is only the feeling of that
(The knocking, the tapping, as if there were
(A barrier of glass, a pane, pain, beyond
(Which one could be sure of neither
(What that is that is there

(Lodged in the words of the book
(Or that there is anything—a species of nothing
So in a circle of ink we sit at a table
Eating the food brought to us by others
To comfort us in the loss of the unlosable
Unfindable
Person, joy of release
Over the bridge by the river
(You can see the tall white steeple
(Against the sky
(Alone near the hill
(Forested and green

5.

Whoever acts with respect will get respect.
Whoever brings sweetness
will be served almond cake.

Love is determined to find its object
In the things scattered about the room
Dolls and photographs
Covered furniture
Ceramic statues unopened mahogany boxes
Clothes in the closet keepsakes in the drawer
Like an open space by the bridge across the river
Not thinking about it but receiving all that's heard
The old remember the long past
In stories
In tales the tragedy recedes
To become a telling

A respect of considering
The ends of stories, power toward which the mind
Inclines, entanglement with focus
(As a scattered light comes in gray in the morning
(Because the back room's enclosed
(There's less light so the room is more quiet
(Left to one's self a music of intention
(That the past—by the big chestnut trees
(Under the snow tunnels as children we dug
(Or the snowmen, we played at having a store
(Because everyone we knew had a store
(With its merchandise to be counted and exchanged
(In that weather at that time
And they believed in the words that reminded them
Said, Pay attention to what has been told
To what has passionately been repeated and sung
What has been sounded out on trumpets
Pay attention to that
When you come in and when you go out
By your arm and on your head
Do not imagine or construct anything
Because you cannot make anything that is not tainted
By wild desire, it is not new
Running along another road
But remember the story of what's been repeated
In the comfort of authority
Be bound in that for the goodness it brings
Being a fine person is that
Held in the flaming words
Of how you are, be that
In the town create people to depend on to use
For the going

Of the entanglement of where you are to go
A white piece of cloth
Only knotted that way
Call it a name but do not say the name
Know it but do not think of it as a name

6.

I can't explain the goings,
or the comings. You enter suddenly,
and I am nowhere again.
Inside the majesty.

You enter suddenly
And I am here again
In a familiar place
(Rugs and a window near the sea
(Openings and closings of the heart
(In the fabric of tasks and relationships
(Ideologies and mutual understandings
(In the early morning quiet, swirl of sound
(Or thought or memory
I do not know how I arrived
In my dream
I stood looking
Only an eye, yellow
The crows in the cages not to be trusted
Ruthless they would peck out an eye
And to them it would be natural
In the teeming market to be careful about what to touch
Or who to stand next to

In this place that is home
Suddenly you're not there
Only if you return
After many years
(In that place
(Which recalls
(Your thought
(Emotions
(Like fear or confusion
(Simply not knowing
(What something meant, that large lawn on it
(With the tall white statue of a comforting Jesus
(The church had placed there—it is still there
(The opaque majestic presence of Jesus a vague threat
(Although normal in someone's world
So it is every day an ordinary world
Then not
It is each time now an explainable sorrow
You do not even think of it, it has a date or a place
Then not—it may erupt on you or it may not
A fragrance in the clothing you are wearing
Or a sheen about the edges of hair
A shimmer in blowing leaves
A stone with an inscription on it in a graveyard
(The person not yet dead but wishing he were
(Making all the necessary preparations
Because death is unexplained
All your life looking over ordinary things
For the opening
In creases or worn spots
Precious stones or objects of desire
In flesh, in food, in flashing images

Always imagining something edged with the look of things
Bordered or crossed, etched or gouged
(Like the time something you had you wanted
(Disappeared suddenly
(Gone utterly
(And it would not return
(No one would make it
(And you felt tears
(Of injustice and loss
(And anger against the hardness
(Of the container of the world
(You knew was not so—and time made that
(Also pass—
(So now speaking there is awareness
(Also of that, it can't be memory
(And words will not speak to who it is
(Other
(And only also
(Myself
(Other and one, another or the unknown one
(As one as the called out to, the named without names
(The never answered
The vegetation's proxy and the furious stone's song
Gapped and fluted borderline dimness
Going around the earth and among people
You cannot be sure of knowing
Cannot plumb the syntax the signs things are
(Some do not believe this
(So many ways to approach the seen
(The sensed—how large to make it how subtle
And surprised you got a grip on what matters you made
Boring into it falling through the hole

But the love not for anyone but everyone
Do not speak of any person or sing psalms
Only stand back bathed in that light
That's not named

7.

By the ocean dark rocks broken by the waves
One rock white with guano where the birds
Have perched endless years
(How time denies time
(How place distances itself from place
What is at the end of the road beyond the hill
Why is it you did not go there
In the past
And now,
Returning
How where you are
On a street full of people you do not know
Why is it you don't stop suddenly
And retrace your steps?
Is memory a feeling that comes at twilight
And when it arrives day's light fades
The seen or the heard wafting by
Like smoke, is contained in a heartbeat
Carried on the breath like a particle
Transported to a world that crushes a world
Only the unsayable jeweled inner life matters

Memory its unconscious glance
Seed of it
Curling or crawling into conception's citadel
So that you know what it is you face
On that street in the city where you live
(In a small town it is very quiet
(No one on the street lined with lawns
(Cars float by where are people going
(In the slow days a languor falls
(From the covering skies
And personal history is fixed
On those public events we share
The large griefs, victories, defeats
Times of new law, disaster, violence, terror
That leave marks on hearts or on buildings
(The house I lived in torn down
(Nothing rebuilt there
(Destroyed to make space for the coming news
(Bare scarred wall

8.

This is not a day for asking questions,
not a day on any calendar.
This day is conscious of itself.
This day is a lover, bread, and gentleness,
more manifest than saying can say.

There are borders between countries or cities
Boundaries of outline between figures
Frames for pictures, skins on people

In the watered sanctuaries of the present
The flow of events suggests starting and stopping
But you can step outside the picture
Where the sun in a corner is blazing
And there consider the strangeness of the past
The public renounced where you are intimate
All the distant thunder of guns
Is your insistence
Is a sound you make in the night
That engenders further pictures
And mows people down like grass
It is only when
You are official to yourself
When you frame outlines onto
The eye of your heart
Calling it this or that
For your protection
Against the terror of time
That the zipping up of the skin begins
The feeling of the past begins to unfold
The cursing that is memory
Recalling this place or that
Vocalizing over again a world
Of insistent occurrence
History isn't that
Memory recedes
Because it's not immediate
No memory
Only the hole inside experience
Where words rush in according to music
And awareness dawns exactly like a sky
Unfolding in the mind

Gradually becoming light
With cloud—streaked red
Memory is the sky, what the imagination
In its reaching toward itself
For confirmation
Or cancellation
Creates or defines
Images of a shining place
Called here
Or a time called now
Unsayable sayings
Vocalized
Collections of names for the nameless
Spoken or sung with cymbal or tambourine
While walking up the steps
Toward the sky
(How the Mayans walked those steep steps
(To narrow rooms at the top
(With crude knives took hearts
(And bled from the penis to repay the debt
(The day makes, the god where flesh had been
(Erased or bled for the world to have been
(His wound
(To be as it is
(So people could rise
(From beds at dawn
(And in their activity of fire or food
(Recreate the beginning of the world
History's not that circle, not vocalized
A mirror making machines possible
Turning imagination into nightmare
Where the moral fiber preserves a dim sense

That can be spoken into
Speaking itself—so memory's that feeling
Around the eyes or lungs
That is not substituted for anything you'd search for
But goes along as the sentence does
(It is not a sentence
(For that would cancel it
(Like a tree that has fallen
(And now dried or eaten by fungi or insects
(Takes on new form producing light
(Not by the energy it makes but in
(Giving up making
(In dying
(Joining past its boundaries
(An addition
A new song which
Replaces itself
How forms of utterance
In tubular catastrophes
Without particular methods
Are buried on the circles
Of history or thought
What you see isn't that
It is extra or compound
(There in the sense of the feel of the street
(Whose size is different
(According to the life you have led
(And what has been lost in the past
(Isn't that there still, the syntax
(Not tortured, verb follows noun
(Looking at something already a memory
(The lines arrive back to themselves

(The story I am telling
(Is a pattern
(Unknown and then known
I do not honor the means of exchange
And it is out of the depth of my feeling this
That it is free—not exchanged—
Not to be measured or valued
But that stripped of its images
It would only be as is
A form of nakedness or immediacy
Nothing between it
To diminish it
Or to be diminished
Things conscious of themselves, alive
Like bread, like wine

9.

There is a community of the spirit.
Join it, and feel the delight
of walking in the noisy street,
and being the noise.

In the boat there is quiet and movement
As the river flows on
The boat's steady or seems to be
Anchored against the streaming waters
It moves with the current
Goes but stops in the same place
In relation to the water
Which is an exchange

With itself
With sky
With mind
Movement with stillness
And in this way on the street
In the city people moving
Like water
The current of their purpose each one
To buy or sell to speak or find pleasure
The pattern to this movement
Shape of coming and going of change
Seen from above the cars and people
Make a perfect mandala
Of time unfolding like a history of memory

10.

Close both eyes
to see with the other eye.

The wise one utters words
But his heart is not stolen
Words are like rocks on a mountain
Therefore you cannot pick them up
Do not hurl them down
For they might pull the mountain apart
Or smash something below
And the splash they make in the waters
When they fly into them from above
Will reverberate too strongly
In the ears of animals

So memorize words engrave them in the ear
Do not allow them the room to be held
Only float by on sound (Music's made
(Beyond the flames of remembering
(Words in the book where you live
(Set to melody they kindle the fire
(That melts the hills like wax
When you arrive remember the landscape
See the sea surrounding the edges of the land
Without crowding it
Coming back again
With great power yet only going so far
(No, sea engulfs the land and eats it
(Land disappears into the sea
(Fire eats earth and it disappears
(Small burnt stone circling endlessly
(In space
Who can draw
A line between
One thing
And another?
Who can find justice
Smudged into that line?
The hole in the heart—fall into it
Forever and speak of it in all that you say
(Words concur with sight,
(Sound, definition's equality or identity
(A cipher or an enigma
So that we can stand down or up
Inspired to form cursory words
Rocks around which waters stream
In the primary sources of the syllable

Letters arise from nowhere, neither body nor mind
Having no form they arise without basis
Instantaneous things hollow and false
Without maker, arising like smoke
Within and without fire
Icons of what is
History and memory together—odes
To perception and the incandescence
Of experience, the "you"
In the "me"
Called out inutterable
In the rock that makes the waters move
In another way, creates a white fury
Where otherwise there is none, place for stalling
So order is imposed
And my foot slips because I do not see the reason
My hand turns against itself
Because I cannot uncover the sky
What I am and know
Flows from what is not I fall
Into the animal
Rise up into the vegetable all days
Reveal and unravel themselves
As the first, as the initial order
Like people wearing gorgeous clothing in a city
Where streets teem with the burdened poor
—Now close the eyes
—See what's on the other side
—Of desire you cannot bear
—To look at

11.

I am not larger than my life
When I return I do not hear myself thinking
Only you there in the shadows
A situation I can only dream about
As my senses condition a world, a past
Repeating in my ear in the thousands
Down that street in the summer humidity
I alone not part of that because there is no life there
That I know about
Nothing I am making there
Only the wonder of the past
Of the person that has been
Closing the book although words go on in other books
Losing the person one loves who now is
Name and memory
Feeling in the limbs
That the person one is isn't as the person one was
In the photos on the wall people long ago gone
Ancestors framed by their perspectives
Exotic past we long to enter, taste
That perfumes this time, is its sweetness,
Redolence, time's aura
How history bleeds into our blood
Like riffling the pages of a book
The unnamable one who lies within thought
Whom I am addressing
Who has written, read,

Erased this poem
Packed the powder of its sound sifted into the whir
Of the wind in the trees, electrical whine, soft sibilance
Of shifting sand or water through sand
The one shot through thought like color
Sinking back all the way toward you
The body a sigh a falling backward into nothing
Into letting go of everything I am or know—
That is the distance to which I aspire
The hills I can see beyond the end of the road
That cannot be traveled

12.

Why do you stay in prison
when the door is so wide open?

In one day many days and in one
Life a million —no words divulge
The meaning in one word—no heart beats
For all the hearts inside me
It is easy to forget everything so that all one makes
Or wants goes to the wind to take it
To another indented life—
In the middle of the town another town
The buildings standing there
The trees whose fingers trace skies
Can be written over again in a book
Words addressed to someone who isn't
A person who presumably was
Or was always a memory of another

Never absent not present except in the book
Whose words it is our duty to repeat
At the proper time
With the proper feeling
To write, sing, post, wear, compel them
As talismans
To be ancestors burned in the words
For whom burning was the words their life arisen
Drifted off as smoke
Vertical and then horizontal east or west
Country by country, language by language
The many things that were not spoken and could not be
Pain made hard as leather and as smooth
I do not imagine what is not so
All that happened
Happened openly
This story's incidents cold and sharp as steel
One hour or half an hour
One day, minute, moment
All that one can see or know
Thoughts, perceptions
(Considering what happens
(Considering wrong and right
(Seeing, hiding and murder
(Family that binds you
(Roving east of the habitable garden
(The land soured and nowhere to plant, to harvest, instead
        shaking
(A fist at the sky, singing in the middle of the night
Only I now following the thread of these pieces
In the fragmented nights
I find shards and slivers and hurl them up

Where they fall I step
Making my lament
And we would be the same people
Have and lose
The same dissolving names
Speaking this language
Playing host to the unsayable
I can tack the photographs
To the wall — here is grandfather and grandmother
Here is mother and father
A man fishing
Smiling and well dressed
In a straw hat
Long ago
The dead and the living
All writing is memory, all memory thought
And all thought memory,
History, every place the unfolding
Of breathing the place engendered and spoke to
And made innocent
By the living and the dying
And the blood calls out
(In the graveyard his grave undiscovered
(The war killed him long ago—but is that so?
(The unloved ones, how do they live and die?
(Who sees that graves are laid for them?
(Who lies next to them?
(Only that the living hearts tie
(To theirs this breathing presence
(Mixing into their dust, that singular
(Presence called one
(Discovered always by surprise

(Only here only now
(Place that does not shrink
(That resurrects the flesh
(In the very body
(In time

13.

You must have shadow and light source both.
Listen, and lay your head under the tree of awe.

All day long I watched the sun move
But it did not move on that day
Instead held its ground in the frozen sky
Slowly the earth began to wobble
Within the distance of space
Heart of the world loosened
Movement and identity
The one that is the many coincided with itself
Just enough warmth stirred
Because of all the years that can be counted
New days came to replace the debris
One new birth each day
Shadow and substance
And the heard, the explained
(All the detail, the upward-arching improvement
(The breaking of what's fixed
(All the impossible doing and motive force
That cannot be said or written only moaned
Touching it
From above the landscape

The hills and forests speaking
Into the rolling places
Farms, wide fields in slanted light
Wide streets of towns east and west of the churning river
And in the shadow of the hills
Cars go by so slowly along highways
Each with wordplay and intention
—then you know nothing can be broken
—look at how one life blends into another
—ball up the longing and the sorrow
And roll it toward the seasons and the storms
Arriving in the seasons
Everything ripens by chance
Taken care of by time's weather
In time's instances seeds come forth
Held in the gnarled palms of unknowing hands

14.

Your way begins on the other side.
Become the sky.
Take an axe to the prison wall.
Escape.
Walk out like someone suddenly born into color.
Do it now.

I saw an old man walk by in the heat
As if lost as if defeated by the deeds of his life
Another man bitter
Smothered by what had been done to him
Sick inside with the fear of love—that it

Cannot be
That it kills
The hospital demolished
The book crumbled
Translation's outmoded (Never can be
(Translated, always revised
(Words' strangeness cannot be mitigated
(Will never understand them's
(Their essential meaning, that they trouble
(Dispossess us in their ambrosial nourishment
New businesses open, new services now offered
And old things are sold
Under new names
They are called old
All this under a sky without clouds
Where scattered birds move east and west
Ink dries on the face of the moon
Children mumble
On the night she died three of them
Stroked her
Weeping
Into the completed quiet
Nothing to give up because no one had
Anything ever, into that scattered sky unfolding
The promises to come
Rage gathers at the corners
Standing against the chair's a doll
Lifelike leaning down onto the chair
To make life welcome
To receive a guest or bear sorrow
If I am here as I can be
Will there be memory of a rainy street

Just arriving in a new city to see a friend
Will I remember childhood, endless
Regress of memory
Repeated in images, phrases, whispers
And can I pile that up and set it aflame
With a single match—all my human feeling
(You'd come out finally into a clearing
(Mountain meadow after days of climbing
(Where you could lay your pack down in the wet grasses
(Dream and remain
(Where it would not matter that you were dead
People of the book, do not forget what binds you
And that to be bound is to be free
Of self, to find the you who is addressed
In the one of the several
Is to know to whom complaints and queries can be made
Know those impulses as music
And play

15.

Stop the words now.
Open the window in the center of your chest,
and let spirit fly in and out.

Abandonment of smoothness in living
Of the effort to get what you want
Be happy, that things will be easy
Not dangle in front
Flow out into fissures (steam coming
(Out, heat and stench, like terror

(But enclosed in the moist
(Feathered space—something I saw
(And remembered, but in
(Remembering is there seeing? In
(Seeing times stutter on themselves
(Stick to one another in a sky-like opening
(To an utter strangeness in being
(One's self, looking, remembering, writing
For a time of remembering
We recall a river
It does not move
This is the river of forgetting—
Drink of its waters
And you will sleep forever
And when you wake
Into a time past forever
You will forget space
You will forget that you have been
You will forget to forget—
Butterfly cocoons hazy on the trees
And bushes, in the summer heat, so much
Drips of life, so many words (and now
(I can see the things and name them
(Each clearer than the last
(Every one another name for my heart
(The wordless fear in the center
Which moon is this?
Is there any law that isn't violated
Inside the feared fearlessness?
Open up the doorway to the staircase
And standing in the stairwell
Prune the plants so you can see through them

Open up the life
So that the life can see a soft hum

16.

Unfold your own myth.

Now they make many objects
Are there known purposes?
Now there are new rooms for the houses
New trails to follow the mountain to the top
One moment suggests another
Each thought or deed a seed
Half remembered half not half true
Half not
A story written in a book in smoke
Myth without a narrative thread
Repeated story
Family saga, mothers and fathers and siblings—
Not that
Not themselves
Only knots in a piece of white cloth
Torqued contractions awaiting release
The tales stutter
All those who are someone
How it came to be, splashes of color
Against the dark background
Which is "one" the same as being "the"
"The" as a particularity of what's general
Pointing it out, pointed out by someone
From a perspective, a location

That is hunkered down into, hunched on
So close that "the" is also "one"
Collapsed into it
As the night without stars
In its utter darkness
Which is moist
Holds all the life of the leaves
Before they are distinguished
Which is the same time—at the
Same time
So all comes and goes—moments
We imagine as if marching
—they have been there
—they will come to be here
—they will recede into a distance elsewhere
But they are not
So they go along stepping in place
To the music, the parents
The painful love
Recounting the ways we were mistaken
Recollecting the unseen connections
Listen to me
For one moment quit being sad
Hear blessings dropping their blossoms
But do not try to gather them
Or even notice them—soon they will
Rot giving rise to further blessings
Received by others
Maybe these will be knotted as a darkness
Against the moon, but even the awful
Terrible twisted lusts of misfortune
Do not cover the justice, true corners

Of seeds coming forth as living what they live
(I do not know how the pattern finds
(Shape, but in the loss of what we
(Most love, that impossibility
(There's release and silence that's
(Peace, things
(That are not produced, are not counted
(Cannot be held
(So open up the hand and let that fly
So many words—how are these
To be distributed and how in the
Many languages there can be
No translations so misunderstanding
Is general
The book
Indecipherable
Upon the table
Floating in the dark

17.

What is love?
Gratitude.

What is hidden
in our chests?
Laughter.

What else?
Compassion.

Today is gray—like a piano that cannot play
But sits massive in the room
Silently disapproving. Take another step.
Fracturing the usual story make today
Yesterday, redeem the seeds
For their sounds making them be at last
As they might all along come forth
Two of them made more of them
Definitions, lip-smackings, covered
Roofs and all bombings and riots
Expected, all horror
—you cannot allow it
—a film on things
--—a point of view
Some things in agreement within that sound
Understanding unfolds straightforwardly —
In the evening when people gather
As they did before, in the morning
In the afternoon
Binding themselves in repeated words
They were told to say they did not know why
Or by whom and repeated them—
A picture double exposed
Of a vacation in a far historical place
Near ruins
Excavations of relics and artifacts
Standing beside the wall
But not the same wall
That held up another house
Because of their being together
(Not any of them but the others in a vertical line
(Backward into time, as if increased accuracy

(More and more close to a source experience
(That came as a wordless sound inside
(Translated into indecipherable words
(That seemed to have meaning but did not
(And were subject to interpretation
(That was always confirmed
(And that caused stones
(To fall out of the sky
There although they did not know how
That was a comfort in their being there
Beside that wall because just then the sun
Set with a warm glow becoming soon
A memory they carried, an image
A word in a book, no, not
An image because it is limited
"One" and "the" like a door in the chest
Opens and shuts, opens and shuts

18.

Be grateful for whoever comes,
because each has been sent
as a guide from beyond.

Happy New Year. In the year's turn
A promise in time—time's hosts
Managed and defended against untime
Surrounds it a miracle
Not in lights and fragments
But in the standing up the sitting down
Outrageous fact

Of walking, talking
Seeing, hearing
Of being the possible unique tree
One is, standing against clouds and waters
One heart that can belie
Love and break open
To keep the world alive there are the few
(One doesn't know who
(Or where slouching
(Only that they ruminate in air
Who go through their days simply
Kindly
Whose hands hold teapots and brooms
And babies' bums
Who stumble along on streets not steady on their feet
With backaches and stomach aches
Poor eyes, dim ears
Ones for whom the spectacle of the world turns
Because of whom others are suffered
To appear and since one doesn't know where
Or which they may be
It is anyone, everyone, be careful to honor them
Lest harm befall you
To be disrespectful of the pivot-point
The reason of being of the world
Of the source-fount of all
Is bad luck so love everything equal
A massive infection often inflicts the body
In the afternoon there is somber light
In the evening and death might come at any time
Turn around where you are
Meet the stranger near the stone still falling

Compromised in being matter inscribed
In the book carried about the room
In a glow of generous complicity
The shout heard there bottomed in a silence
Such as the world can never know (animals
(Do not climb trees, breezes do not stir
(People have
(Nothing to say
The hush this brings, the charged words repeated
A thousand years
So that they become non words
That are free
Of meaning's weight
Like orchestrated moans
In history's wings
Not damaged by being lip-read or breath-
Read but brought down low
(Belly's the place
(Bringing fire to earth
(Bringing water to air
It's not sophisticated to plow earth there
With a tree branch pulled by oxen
To open up the collar of the shirt
Letting in air and dirt
The endless toil on the earth's flat plain
Whereas time, like an arrow, goes on swift
And deep
At any point wounded, blood-red lives
In concatenation's splendor
The sacrifice to be born and live
A moment to go

19.

Whoever finds love
beneath hurt and grief

disappears into emptiness
with a thousand new disguises.

I'd still have only one history
I'd still fall at the end of the day
All my luck turned pain
Memory distorted by pressure of the present
Brought me a bright red cloth I allowed
To be addressed to the kings of the province
So many sick with grief, stopped up
Like bottles full of stones
In enraptured entrances of the past
Weighs down on here, that painting
Of hell the damned tortured
In their bodies twisted
Nothing allowed
Only held fast in their places
Forever with heavy stones on their backs
And flames at their sides and behind
Naked and without protection
Going down come up
Like the sun does (it doesn't)
Come back
Find summer after winter
Flowers after frost
Your white hair the hair of your daughter
(She who in the first shine of youth

(Wandered close to the spring
(Wanted being pulled by the future in desire
(Had in her hair that aroma of love
Hair of your mother so handsome
Coming into the country
Losing touch with fashion
Having been by the confusion lost to herself
So not knowing how to hold in her hand
Any life to be known but running
Not stopping to stay aligning herself with a man
(A man and a woman cleave together
(As two parts of a whole sought in anger or fear
(That they can't be happy, that cruelty
(Begets cruelty that there's damage
(In being damaged
But like the hush below the blast of the sound
Because terrible and joyful at the same time
(Anything that way, the light and the weighty
(Any feeling also another feeling, all persons
(Other persons stretched toward
(Themselves
There's a feeling in letting go
Of loss of hurt of defeat
Freedom in the final release
Of possibility
Knowing that here's where one is
Hidden in one
In the words the book celebrated
Ark of the covered promise

20.

But what can stay hidden?
Love's secret is always lifting its head
out from under the covers,
"Here I am!"

All laid out and bare
Wrapped in the names of things
That are not delicate, not sophisticated
No secret held
Concealed and cherished
It's so plain it's indecipherable
(As not to be so, untellable
Is revealed at all points
Remaining therefore the greatest mystery
To stand up sit down speak or look
Out onto the lake shore
To see geese fly by
And know that
Time's parade's not marked
In memory or expectation
But that (like throwing into the air
(A handful of petals
(How they fall in patterns according to air or weight
(The upward thrust of hand or eye
(Wish and love's enthusiasm
All's lost in knowing's syntax
Looped back to the trailhead
A forty year poem returned
To its first line, its first impulse
Ocean appears a diamond or an emerald

With dense clouds in ranks
Hovering close
Every gesture revealing
Nothing ever not to be seen
All my scandals open-toed and relaxed
Like waterfalls
However it meant it to be
It is
(Statement or government, precedent or
(Antecedent neither in front nor behind
(Is anything solid or firm
You are, it is, the me of it's not fixed in place
Can climb this mountain or that
Thunder your miracles over the horizons
Bridge between here and there's quite true
Suspended according to natural law
Unrepeatable coincidences
People know because
Mind's bow lets fly
Great emptiness, the great unspeakable you
In this or that
You in me
One in many
(The way they say
(Is not the one
(Living fire nor its air
(Floats by over those waters
(The bridge doesn't go there
(Only at the end unthinkable when you greets you
(When one returns to itself when one's here
(Absolutely
Courses in the commerce of the statement

Which is a question
The ever-possible asking, forever-asking
Ripening of the heart like a clear bell
Ringing over the waters
On whose sound those geese soar
Who aren't going or coming anywhere
But crying freedom in the clear knowing going
According to conditions and true laws
Which are not coming from outside
But from the inner actual shapes
The cold high movement of the calling

21.

A great silence overcomes me,
and I wonder why I ever thought
to use language.

In the early morning on the road's a deer
By the side of the road frightened
In the light of the headlamp bolting up
The hill and falling down all her weight
Of a sudden into the car going by
And colliding there with a crash of the mirror
That mirror's face cracked
Person's objectified as mime of myself fractured
To worry about but is only reflected light's shadow
Shimmering as if mirror's a lake
Or river to be crossed
Back and forth east and west daily all the days
Of the past

Seeing I am he but he is not me
No objects only subjects, subject
Nothing to pick up only something to put down
That is pressed upon
Broken finally—altogether smashed
In a shower of painted glass
Next a possum there
In the road grooming
In the middle of the road in the dark
(This in the past, is memory
Diamond eyes
Ocean eyes deep, indecipherable
(Such subjects without reflection
Tree-leaf eyes
(Each one distinguished but not another
Like a beast from another world lost
In this one the beast
On the road I saw
When the car swerved
Drunk I was and did not know what
I saw, followed
Confusion, reaching out with hands to want it
As something real it is not — it's the mind's
Subject startling possum
With such metallic tail and bald
Grayish pink, slow, not jumping like a deer with that
          ardor
Going off the road seeing this thing slowly moving
Off the road
And falling backward with a crash
Into the present fright not knowing what I am
But not moving, not worried, only grooming

Not moving, not looking
Out
With ocean-diamond eyes in the reflected light

22.

Your old life was a frantic running
from silence.

The speechless full moon
comes out now.

I ask
Why did I begin?
What did I hope for?
Where did I think to be going with my tubes and tins?
However these questions step back into myself
Toward the mind's source stream of forgetting
Remembering the first cloud there in the morning
Catching the morning's dawning piling up
One cloud on another as day's light glows on—
Always the answer which is a question
Not wanting an answer
A question that's pure wanting
And nothing to be wanted
Released to it like wind
Up and then gone in less than an instant
(Is this what I am repeating
(That someone has said?
All of myself disappearing
(How do I know? I do not know

(So that in the pure laughter of poverty
(Of the deprivation of myself within myself
(Like a cabinet inside a cabinet
(Of all objects that the senses know
And I read "Abraham knew Sarah"
And the knowing made the issue Isaac
Which was abandoned, offered
This is a music
Because I have forgotten the episodes
All the stories of my life—what happened?
(And returning to the river
(Crossed daily to the battle
(Took place there
(As the fort guarding
(The river lasting two years
(Did those things happen other than
(That there is now
(There is here and there
(Knotted into the cloth
(You are not in good hands
(Hands holding what is thin air
Yes I will tell you a story but only so that you
Can forget the story
Words bitten into paper to be read
Following along with finger or lips
Crawling ranks of ink clouds
To be followed like light or laughter
Around the room all rise and follow ink in new lines
In the exigency of that or the emotion of someone's
Story to float inside
So the commentary should reduce the weight
Making the meaning to be opposite

To subdue the terror and bitter enigmas
Substituting air light or wonder
That floats off from the page
Black lines and dots entering the sky
Brings tears those repeated words of the story
That are free and do not mean anything now
Do not erase the heart or punish it
Because they are erased open it
Through the tales that are music only now
(What
(Could that
(Be what
(Could those
(Signify it is not
(What occurs
(As past or present
(It is another
(Something
(Else

23.

Instead of being so bound up with everyone,
         Be everyone.

Bound up in life's knot
Letting them be
So bound as to remain
Those who are gone, inexist let them be we
Say
Bound in those bindings (bindings of

(Isaac
(Laughter —bindings, comical
(Life that is absolutely
(Given
(As absolutely
(Taken
(Ripped away
(Sacrificed
(Given over
(As sacrifice in time, he said
So Anne's gone yet bound in the sorrow
Of her husband
In the passion of her sister
In the anguish and terror
Of her daughter
In the struggle to deny the loosing
Of the knot
Cloth flowing in wind freely
How is it we're everyone already?
Loneliness isn't possible since
All's draped with the cloth
Empty or full because thin
Is everywhere isolated, included
So not really there
As anything or anyone
Moon over pond, paper over rock
Mind over matter
And the character in the story in the line
Is someone else now
No image only darkness ever was
Struggle inscribed in love's book
As the woman said who could see the future

"It's like that, not that but
Like that, that way the past
Folds forward and back
Making patterns in tea leaves"
My body disappears into yours in sight
Perception's continuous suicide
Even mind and thought
Isn't of myself
Thin, it waves in the moonlight
Knotted
Inevitable, ineluctable
Crawls out to an edge of light
And illuminated bursts into view
As it would not in the dark
Baby's fingers pull down the moon
Her forceful desire
Like a ball bouncing on a bubbling stream
Is everywhere at once bound so completely
There
As to be entirely free
Never alone as long as it is
A question
A wanting toward
A one addressed that isn't

24.

Everything has to do with loving and not loving.
This night will pass.
Then we have work to do.

On the ruin is evidence
And without evidence we would be nothing
Pack up all sorrow of longing—it is illusion
That which is the heart's not far
From the ruined wall with its suggestion of a thinkable
          past
To remember conquerors and their systems
Of food production, implements, the pagination
That made rulers of them
Holding the higher aspiration
Vision manufactured out of leisure
Time on their hands
Time
On their hands so cultivate lands
With surplus now possibility
Not like birds eating all day long
Simply no oppression
Not even death as a known disappointment
Because no ruins to view only nests year by year
Abandoned or reused this is now
In the past of one person's grandeur
Not in having been what was done
Its doing and its record
But in the fact of its having been as record
Exact having been
A thinkable past that moves like smoke
Across human skies
Thin and wavering
Bound up in life as if over again
Which you can see there in the ruin
Of an old church or wall
(A wall only

(Barely standing
(In the middle
(Of the night
Whatever is real or not there is always tomorrow
And is today
Always facing a direction to go in
And daily living to be provided for
Which are clothing and eating and cooking
And cleaning it up there are
Eliminations and wastes
Turns in the road bumps
Seen and felt impressions
Reflections in mirrors
Of minds, memories
There are twinnings and bindings of the fabric
This must be life or it must be death
(Death good practice for life
(Or life good practice for dying
(In the pattern of the fabric a tear
(That's part of the pattern
Despite this I understand nothing,
Nothing and am what you have made
It is Greek or it is Jewish—Greek
Small myth of family and suffering
Unspoken constellations in one big night
Little eddies or currents in the pool of light
Behind things, ruin of all that could have been's
Just how this only
Is appreciated
Why always in moonlight?
Is there another planet somewhere
With this kind of moonlight

And ponds
And trees like these
And bushes like these, tangles of living?
Or just one like this in black space anywhere?

25.

Pale sunlight,
pale the wall.

Love moves away.
The light changes.

I need more grace
than I thought.

These days of the long shadow
Days of the long sun these
Shorter days days
Of remembering days
Friendship sustains
Even in absence what stays
Constant grows
Making one identity
(As if
(Things
(Did not
(Come to pass and
(Pass then new ones
(Come flashing up out of the dark
(Sparks illuminating flaming words

(Grasped as true
So I remember past days
In the warmth of friendly concern
And love showers onto the scene
A forgiving glow of persimmon
That everything be as it is
And is all right (leaves fall, fruit swells)
Things empty themselves
All yesterdays between today
And what's repeated now and again repeated
True by virtue of its being repeated
As a music in the structure of what is
Not historical
Because this is what's needed
Story of the past for the present
For friendship warm as wine
And magnify our days
Remembering the story
Not as what was
But as structure of now's mind to be itself
Shape of a nameless present
For myself
To appear here for its value
Every part perfectly fit
Like a long shelf of beautiful books
All stood straight up and ready to fall open
Pale day
Every day
Pale saying in a book
Cracking its bindings
Shedding its leaves in season
Into this

Now that
Grace to be
Written
Opened then folded back
Grace to see
What's in the hand
Here then absent
In the storm on the land
Cloud-fate to be laughter
Pale day
All day
Pale night's might

26.

*Awe is the salve
that will heal our eyes.*

And winter's the time
To look back
I was born in the snow so snow's home
White covering shape as though all things
Are one color bearing one flame
Water's plume, cooling water
Trees covered with snow
Earth under the trees covered with snow
(Only some fresh footprint of shoe or animal paw
(Some bird-foot criss-cross in the feathery
(Snow
I am born once then again
Plunged into the snow that unrolls the eyes

Back to the snows
Of yesterday...
So the heard's the snow of hearing
A fox barking or a jay squawking
Sound of stream or steam or wind or plane
Overheard not names but heard for no one's
Listening only the sound goes in, turning
The eighth stage of mental functioning
The eighth consciousness reverted, mind
Stepped back apace all's redeemed all of them
In the desert listening (being listening
Swaying in the heart's wind like young trees
How there isn't a story to be put together
And evaluated
(Sixth consciousness
(Doesn't identify
(Seventh consciousness
(Doesn't remember or judge
But hearing the sound of water rushes by
(This is also sound of words in a book
(Sound of words on a page also words
(Spoken in sleep at the beginning
(Mouth forces grunting and sorrow
(Nonwords spoken even when
(Mind's purposes to hold anything solid
(Fleeting like clouds dissolving
(And there's no sense anymore of words
(Only sounds to be repeated senseless when
(Speech can't be repeated when thought's
(Impossible and self's forgot those music
(Words flow on, ancient and repeated
(Having come from elsewhere, the awe,

(Fear but not fear of running away
(From a crushing embrace but fear
(As a trembling of the windpipe
(With the ecstasy of hearing
(The human music
(With its blood and pulse
(Walking in the garden in the wind of the day
Here—bell's sound
Here—wooden board beaten, drum beaten
Here—footsteps and bird whistles, laughter
And the murmuring low voices passing through
Air
Ticking clock and pen scratch
In the silence
Only listening
(Not hearing anything
Absorbed in that as if a stairwell
Into the water of the mind
Down to the bottom of it but not standing
On the bottom instead
Suspended
Part way down
In the clarity of it like a bell
Tone dying out gradually over the water
Of absence
Of the once-was in its isness as that
The absence as clothing of it
As making it appear or disappear
To be hidden within it
So it arises in the ceasingness of arising
Is purity in impurity of its pureness
Is only void-sound in its overlapping

In its not being named or written
Moist and reverberating in the ear
(If there were no ear what sound
(Is here—in "if," in "were"
(Such sound as may be
(Eternally eternally propounded

27.

Which is worth more, a crowd of thousands,
or your own genuine solitude?
Freedom, or power over an entire nation?

A little while alone in your room
will prove more valuable that anything else
that could ever be given you.

Yes yes I know
To be alone is best to dance
Before the mirror naked wondering
Who is this what strange
Limbs these are to be dancing like that
Lifting the palms toward the sky
Surrounded by trees, lake, rock
Let go of being tired of it see your room
As an ocean go through its waves and hillocks
Spume of foam to the earthy part
Eating the fruit you want with its seed of tomorrow
That need not be
No longer imitating or keeping standards
Not conforming or forming

But showering petals into the air above
While walking in procession (mind
(Surrendered to the theme of your living
(To the shape heart made
(As it lay down in the suggestible
(Pine needle cover making a
(Depression for an instant that sprang back
(To be as it was all along soon before you
(Came and the trees burned or dropped
(More needles, raining them down quietly
(For a thousand years as you came and went
(Many times
Some of them gathered food or hunted
These were the quiet ones, few on the land
Others grew food according to what
They noticed or dreamed
In the dream they were eaten
Into the world consumed by heat
And more children came crowding in
Needing food and making sounds to be listened to
Whose cries were heard in the imagination
That saw precisely what was not, projected a world
That was not, that became what was by the force
Of the dream and the driven fear
So in the absence of food
There's activity
The gathering and the growing of dreams
In its repeating making a crowd of us
We must be in a crowd of them

28.

*To change
a person must face
the dragon of his appetites
with another dragon,
the life energy
of the soul.*

Waves of what went before's momentum
Slosh onto the shores of now
Just as a stone dropped from on high
Will fall
Till it lands
So my passion's
Not my fault only I can
Let it fall
Not bat it around too much with a crude club
Till it beat my head
Unconscious
Desire rises up and falls
Life's pulse and flow
Makes beauty to be in sensation
All void and gone in the peaceful doing
Of what's so in a life in a time and a place
So all desire's satisfaction of itself
To be enjoyed and followed
Not as what's grasped and poked into being
(Which never can be but only a thrusting
(Rapping at the door that's only opened
(By a free wind gently wafting
But as what floats on mind's waters

Anything the senses mend
In sensation pushing or thrusting aside
Holding what's thin air
As if it were a knotted cloth
As if a thread to be followed to be woven into a garment
That couldn't be but only crashing necessity
Weighs down, old mistake
Never stopping any of that (all the words
(That came to me that I want to let them
(Come to me that they can make a circle
(To be closed knit time past to be present
(Bridge future in the darkened windows of time
Only allowing the openness of it (like a door
(Open and you can go in
(Shutting it behind you
To enjoy itself by putting aside the luggage and the broom
Making something quiet in the room
So that the sound opens as the soil opens
And you can plant
Darkness

29.

Every part of you has a secret language.
Your hands and your feet say what you've done.
And every need brings in what's needed.
Pain bears its cure like a child.
Having nothing produces provisions.
Ask a difficult question,
and the marvelous answer appears.

Norman Fischer is a Zen Buddhist priest and teacher, who lived and worked in Buddhist monastic centers most of his life. After serving a term as co-abbot of the San Francisco Zen Center, he founded the Everyday Zen Foundation (www. EverydayZen.org), dedicated to sharing Zen teachings and practice widely with the world. His ongoing writing practice has resulted in many readings, collaborations, performances, and publications over the years. His most recent poetry books are *Success* (Singing Horse Press, 2000) and *Slowly But Dearly* (Chax, 2004). His most recent Buddhist book is *Taking Our Places: the Buddhist Path to Truly Growing Up* (Harper San Francisco, 2004).

Singing Horse Press Titles

Charles Alexander, *Near Or Random Acts*, 2004, $15
Julia Blumenreich, *Meeting Tessie.* 1994, $6.00
Linh Dinh, *Drunkard Boxing.* 1998, $6.00
Norman Fischer, *Success.* 1999, $14.00
Phillip Foss, *The Ideation.* 2004, $15.00
Eli Goldblatt, *Without a Trace.* 2001, $12.50
Mary Rising Higgins, *)cliff TIDES((.* 2005, $15.00
Karen Kelley, *Her Angel.* 1992, $7.50
Kevin Killian & Leslie Scalapino, *Stone Marmalade.* 1996, $ 9.50
Hank Lazer, *The New Spirit. 2005, $14.00*
McCreary, Chris & Jenn, *The Effacements / a doctrine of signatures*
        2002, $12.50
David Miller, *The Waters of Marah.* 2002, $12.50
Andrew Mossin, *The Epochal Body.* 2004, $15.00
Harryette Mullen, *Muse & Drudge.* 1995, $12.50
Harryette Mullen, *S*PeRM**K*T.* 1992, $8.00
Paul Naylor, *Playing Well With Others,* 2004, $15.00
Gil Ott, *Pact.* 2002, $14.00
Heather Thomas, *Practicing Amnesia.* 2000, $12.50
Rosmarie Waldrop, *Split Infinities.* 1998, $14.00
Lewis Warsh, *Touch of the Whip.* 2001, $14.00

Singing Horse Press books are available online at singinghorsepress.
com or through Small Press Distribution (800) 869-7553 or on the
web at www.spdbooks.org.